W9-AHK-136

DOGS

by Meish Goldish

Consultant: Wilma Melville, Founder
National Disaster Search Dog Foundation

BEARPORT
PUBLISHING

New York, New York

WITHDRAWN

Charles County Public Library
P.D. Brown Memorial Library
301-645-2864   301-843-7688
www.ccplonline.org

Special thanks to Wilma Melville who founded the:
National Disaster Search Dog Foundation
206 N. Signal Street, Suite R
Ojai, CA 93023
(888) 4K9-HERO
www.SearchDogFoundation.org

The Search Dog Foundation is a not-for-profit organization that rescues dogs, gives them professional training, and partners them with firefighters to find people buried alive in disasters. They produce the most highly trained search dogs in the nation.

Credits

Cover and Title Page, © Photodisc/Fotosearch; Cover (background), © PhotoEuphoria/Istockphoto.com; 4, Courtesy of Judi Bayly; 5, Courtesy of Judi Bayly; 6, © Andrea Booher/FEMA News Photo; 7, © Debrah Tosch/Search Dog Foundation; 8, © Debrah Tosch/Search Dog Foundation; 9, © Mike Rieger/FEMA/Getty Images/Newscom.com; 10, © AP Images/pa-ho; 11, © Jim Gensheimer, San Jose Mercury News; Copyright San Jose Mercury News. All rights reserved; 12, Courtesy of Bill Proulx; 13, Courtesy of Bill Proulx; 14, Courtesy of William Munoz; 15, Courtesy of William Munoz; 16, © AFP PHOTO/HO/SCIENCE/Susanne Baus/Newscom.com; 17, © REUTERS/Manuela Hartling; 18, © Courtesy of Dr. Stanley Coren; 19T, © Andraž Cerar/Shutterstock; 19B, © age fotostock/SuperStock; 22, © Kim Karpeles/age fotostock/SuperStock; 23, © The Granger Collection, New York; 24, © FogStock LLC/IndexOpen; 25T, © John Mitchell/Photolibrary/Oxford Scientific; 25B, © Daniel Cox/Photolibrary/Oxford Scientific; 26, © Ken Weaver/America 24-7/Getty Images; 27, © Courtesy of Adam Siegel; 28L, © Ralph Reinhold/IndexOpen; 28R, © Chin Kit Sen/Shutterstock; 29, Courtesy of Del Monte Food Corporation.

Publisher: Kenn Goin
Project Editor: Adam Siegel
Creative Director: Spencer Brinker
Photo Researcher: Beaura Kathy Ringrose
Original Design: Dawn Beard Creative

Library of Congress Cataloging-in-Publication Data

Goldish, Meish.
  Dogs / by Meish Goldish ; consultant, Wilma Melville.
      p. cm.—(Smart animals!)
  Includes bibliographical references and index.
  ISBN-13: 978-1-59716-368-2 (library binding)
  ISBN-10: 1-59716-368-6 (library binding)
  1. Working dogs—Juvenile literature. I. Title. II. Series.

  SF428.2.G64 2007
  636.7—dc22

                          2006032552

Copyright © 2007 Bearport Publishing Company, Inc. All rights reserved. No part of this publication may be reproduced in whole or in part, stored in a retrieval system, or transmitted in any form or by any means, electronic, mechanical, photocopying, recording, or otherwise, without written permission from the publisher.

For more information, write to Bearport Publishing Company, Inc., 101 Fifth Avenue, Suite 6R, New York, New York 10003. Printed in the United States of America.

10 9 8 7 6 5 4 3 2 1

Contents

Telephone Hero

Judi Bayly was in trouble. Her oxygen machine, which helped her breathe, stopped working. The machine's alarm went off, but Judi was asleep. That's when her **service dog**, Lyric, came to the rescue. As she had been trained to do in this kind of emergency, Lyric made a telephone call.

▲ Lyric

The Irish setter knocked the phone off the hook. Then, with her paws, she pressed buttons that dialed 911. When an operator answered, Lyric barked into the phone. The operator immediately sent help. Lyric had saved Judi's life!

▲ **Judi called her dog "my own live-in lifesaver."**

Service dogs can be trained to pull wheelchairs, turn lights on and off, open doors and cabinets, and fetch items for people.

Dog to the Rescue

Lyric is just one of many smart dogs trained to handle different kinds of emergencies. On September 11, 2001, airplanes crashed into the World Trade Center in New York City. The Twin Towers collapsed, and thousands of people were killed.

After the World Trade Center attack, more than 300 dogs helped search for victims.

Rescue workers raced to the scene. Their job was extremely difficult. People were buried under tall piles of **debris** and twisted steel. Luckily, Abby, a Labrador retriever, was also there to help. Abby used her training as a disaster search dog to look for survivors among the **rubble**.

▲ Abby, a four-year-old Labrador retriever, worked with her handler, Debra Tosch, at the World Trade Center site.

The Gift of Smell

Search dogs like Abby are a huge help at disaster sites. With the help of their noses, they can **pinpoint** where someone is buried. This skill is very helpful to rescue workers who often need to reach trapped people quickly to save them from dying.

▲ **Abby searching for victims after the World Trade Center attack**

Abby can smell a human's **scent** deep in the ground. She sniffs the air, picks up a scent, and follows it to its source. She barks to say, "I found someone!" Abby puts not only her brain to work, but her powerful nose as well.

▲ Search and rescue dogs are trained to enter dark tunnels and walk on shaky surfaces without fear.

All dogs have an amazing sense of smell. They can smell up to 10,000 times better than a human. They can smell a person buried in rubble 30 feet (9 m) deep!

Doctor Dog

Some dogs use their powerful sense of smell to become medical detectives. Doctors hope to use these smart animals to help them find deadly diseases. Breeze is a golden retriever who has been taught to **detect** skin cancer in humans.

▲ **Tangle is a cocker spaniel. Like Breeze, Tangle uses his strong sense of smell to recognize the scent of cancer.**

To train Breeze, her owner placed cancer cells in a tube. The dog smelled them to learn their scent. After her training, Breeze smelled the skin of seven patients. She touched her nose to the exact spot where cancer was located in each person. One time she even detected cancer that the doctor's tests had missed!

Some medical detective dogs can identify lung cancer by smelling a person's breath.

◀ **Kobi is another dog who was trained to detect cancer.**

Dog Cop

Breeze's smart sniffing wouldn't surprise other people who work with dogs. Just ask police officer Bill Proulx. He spends his day **patrolling** the streets with Bruno, a German shepherd. At a crime scene, Bruno is able to sniff a shoe mark and then follow that scent to find the **suspect**.

Officer Bill ▶ Proulx and his dog, Bruno

Bruno was trained at a police dog **academy**. He learned how to climb tall walls, and how to bite and hold a suspect on **command**.

Bruno is very good at following orders. When Officer Proulx says, "Break," Bruno lets go of the suspect's arm. When he says, "Watch," Bruno barks loudly. This scares the suspect, so the police can easily handcuff him.

▲ **Officer Proulx helped train Bruno for his job as a police dog.**

A police dog can smell a human's scent a quarter of a mile (.4 km) away.

Leading the Way

Dogs can be trained to find survivors at disaster sites and catch criminals. Can they also help **disabled** people? The answer is yes. Irah is a guide dog that helps Don Simmonson, who is blind. Don holds on to Irah's **harness** as the dog safely leads him to work.

▲ **Irah, a golden retriever, guides his owner, Don, across the street.**

Irah was carefully trained to guide blind people. He learned when to stop at street corners and when it was safe to cross. Irah also learned when to disobey an order. Don may tell Irah to walk at a green light. However, if a car is coming, Irah will not move. He is smart enough to know that it's not safe.

◀ Irah

Dogs don't see colors as clearly as humans. However, they are much better than people at seeing motion.

A Way with Words

Like Bruno and Irah, most dogs can be taught to understand words. This skill is one sign of an animal's intelligence. Many scientists think the average dog can learn about 100 words. If that's true, then Rico is a word champion. This border collie has learned more than 200 words.

▲ Rico

To train Rico, his owners gave him many toys. They taught him the name for each one. When they said a name, Rico learned to pick out the right toy!

Rico doesn't just memorize words, however. He can **reason**, too. One time his owners placed a new toy among his old ones. Then they said the new toy's name. Rico was able to pick it out of the pile right away.

Rico's vocabulary is equal to that of other smart animals, such as dolphins, sea lions, and parrots, which have been trained to understand words.

▲ **Rico and his toys**

Who Is the Smartest?

Dogs like Rico make scientists wonder: Just how smart are dogs? How do they compare to humans? Dr. Stanley Coren, a **psychologist** and dog trainer, says dogs are nearly as smart as a two-year-old child.

▲ **Dr. Stanley Coren and his dogs**

Dr. Coren studied more than 100 dog **breeds**. He put them in order according to their intelligence. More than 200 dog **obedience** judges helped with the study. They rated the dogs on how well they were able to carry out commands, as well as their ability to use their training.

Dr. Coren's 10 Smartest Dogs

1. Border collie
2. Poodle
3. German shepherd
4. Golden retriever
5. Doberman pinscher
6. Shetland sheepdog
7. Labrador retriever
8. Papillon
9. Rottweiler
10. Australian cattle dog

▲ **Dr. Coren rated the border collie as the most intelligent type of dog.**

The Afghan hound was at the bottom of Dr. Coren's list of smartest dogs.

Body Language

Dogs are smart enough to understand words spoken by people. Yet how do dogs **communicate** with one another or with people? One way is by using **body language**.

Playful Dog

If a dog wags its tail wildly, that means "I like you a lot!"

tail up

ears up

mouth open, tongue showing

lowered front end

▲ This dog is saying, "I want to play!"

A dog can use its ears, eyes, mouth, and tail to send different messages. For example, a dog may pull its ears back, tuck in its tail, curl its lips, and wrinkle its nose. These body movements show that the dog is frightened. If a dog's ears are straight up, that shows the dog is paying attention.

Frightened Dog

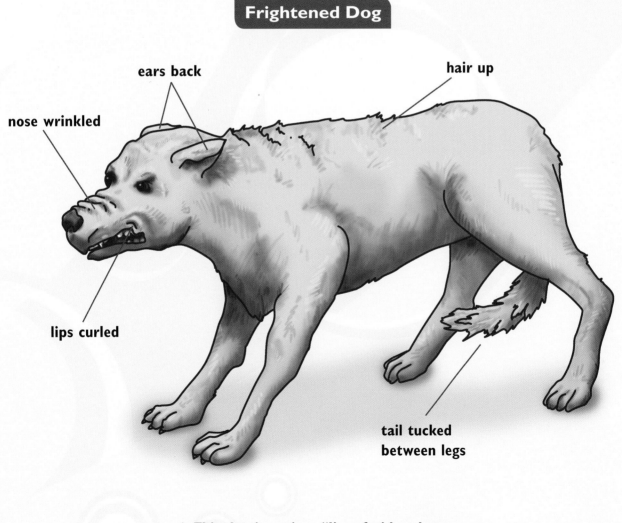

nose wrinkled

ears back

hair up

lips curled

tail tucked between legs

▲ **This dog is saying, "I'm afraid and may bite you to defend myself."**

21

A Famous Experiment

People can teach dogs different skills. Yet the animals also learn from experience. In the early 1900s, a Russian scientist named Ivan Pavlov discovered this fact while studying how dogs eat.

Every time Pavlov gave a group of dogs food, they would drool. One day Pavlov walked into the room without any food. Yet the dogs still drooled. Why?

A dog's mouth naturally begins to water when the animal smells food.

Pavlov realized that the dogs had made a connection. When they saw him coming, they expected food. So they automatically drooled.

Pavlov conducted more tests. He rang a bell before feeding the dogs. Soon they were drooling just upon hearing the bell. The dogs had made another connection. They knew the sound of the bell meant that it would soon be time to eat.

▲ **Ivan Pavlov (right) shows his dog experiment to medical students.**

Wild Dogs

Dogs that are kept as pets or trained to help people are **domesticated** animals. There are other kinds of smart dogs, however, that are wild animals.

The coyote is a wild dog that plays tricks. It will leap about to get the attention of a bird. A second coyote then sneaks up from behind and grabs the bird for a tasty treat!

Wild Dogs Around the World

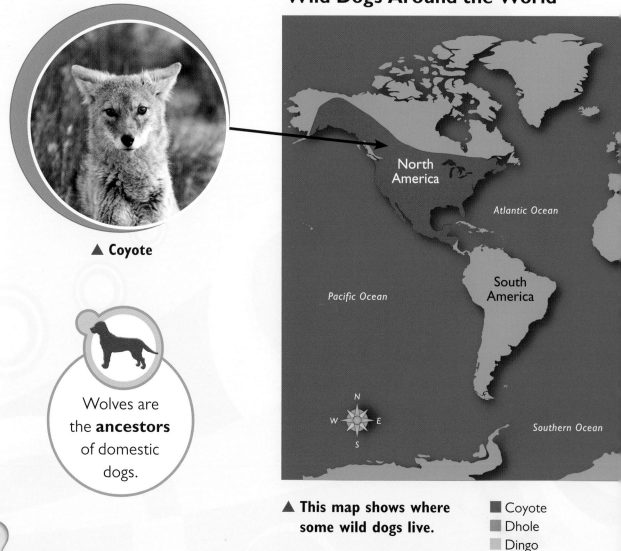

▲ **Coyote**

Wolves are the **ancestors** of domestic dogs.

North America

Atlantic Ocean

Pacific Ocean

South America

Southern Ocean

▲ **This map shows where some wild dogs live.**

■ Coyote
■ Dhole
■ Dingo

The dhole (DOHL) also uses teamwork. It communicates by barking and growling. Hunting in a group of 20 or more, these wild dogs kill large animals such as deer.

The dingo is a wild dog, too. It has a clever way to stay safe. If an enemy approaches, the dingo pretends to be dead. The enemy is fooled and goes away.

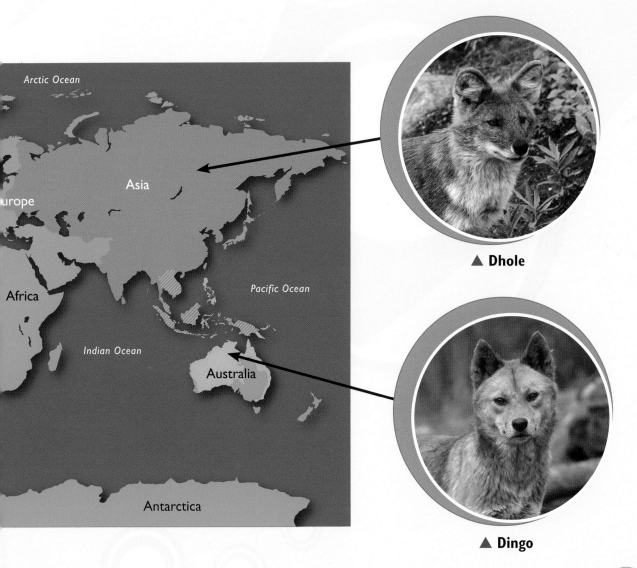

▲ **Dhole**

▲ **Dingo**

Loving and Loyal

Every day, all around the world, dogs are helping people. Some may be searching for survivors after a disaster. Others are sniffing for criminals or cancer. Some dogs are helping blind people get to work.

▲ **This dog has been trained to round up a flock of sheep on a farm.**

Yet no matter how dogs help humans, their owners usually care about them for a different reason. These brainy animals make great pets and **companions**. For thousands of years, dogs have made their owners proud of them for being loyal, loving, and, of course, smart!

There are about 60 million dogs in the United States. Many of them are working dogs, but even more are simply pets.

Just the Facts

There are more than 150 dog breeds.
Here are the largest and the smallest.

	Irish Wolfhound	**Chihuahua**
Height (at shoulder)	30–35 inches (76–89 cm)	4–6 inches (10–15 cm)
Weight	105–140 pounds (48–63.5 kg)	2–6 pounds (0.9–2.7 kg)
Life Span	about 6–8 years	about 12–16 years
Coat	rough and wiry	long-haired or short-haired
Type of Dog	hound	toy dog

More Smart Dogs

The owners of Oscar, a four-year-old beagle, moved from Niagara Falls, New York, to Indianapolis, Indiana. They left Oscar behind with their grandson. Seven months later, Oscar showed up at the family's new home in Indianapolis. The dog had walked more than 500 miles (805 km)! No one knows how he found his way, since he had never left Niagara Falls before.

When an 11-year-old girl became trapped in a snowstorm, a Newfoundland puppy named Villa made a brave rescue. Hearing the girl's cries for help, Villa leaped over a tall fence to reach her. She walked around the area to clear the snow. Then she positioned herself so the girl could grab her neck. Villa pulled the girl out of the deep snow and led her home.

▲ Villa

Glossary

academy (uh-KAD-uh-mee) a school that teaches special subjects or skills

ancestors (AN-sess-turz) family members who lived a long time ago

body language (BOD-ee LANG-gwij) body movements used to share information

breeds (BREEDZ) types of a certain animal

command (kuh-MAND) an order given to a person or animal

communicate (kuh-MYOO-nuh-kate) to pass on ideas, thoughts, or feelings to others

companions (kuhm-PAN-yuhnz) animals or people with whom one spends time

debris (duh-BREE) scattered pieces of something that has been wrecked or destroyed

detect (di-TEKT) to discover or notice something

disabled (diss-AY-buhld) unable to easily do everyday things because of an illness or injury

domesticated (duh-MESS-tuh-*kate*-id) bred and tamed animals for use by humans

harness (HAR-niss) a device attached to an animal that allows people to hold on to the animal

obedience (oh-BEE-dee-uhns) doing what one is told to do

patrolling (puh-TROHL-ing) walking around an area to keep it safe

pinpoint (PIN-*point*) to locate the exact place

psychologist (sye-KOL-uh-jist) a person who studies people's minds and behavior

reason (REE-zuhn) to think in a way that makes sense

rubble (RUHB-uhl) piles of things that have been broken or destroyed

scent (SENT) the smell of something or someone

service dog (SUR-viss DAWG) a dog that is trained to help people who can't get around easily on their own

suspect (SUH-spekt) someone who is thought to have committed a crime

30

Bibliography

Coile, D. Caroline, Ph.D. *How Smart Is Your Dog? 30 Fun Science Activities with Your Pet.* New York: Sterling (2003).

Coren, Stanley. *The Intelligence of Dogs: A Guide to the Thoughts, Emotions, and Inner Lives of Our Canine Companions.* New York: Free Press (2006).

Owens, Carrie. *Working Dogs.* Rocklin, CA: Prima Publishing (1999).

Singer, Marilyn. *A Dog's Gotta Do What a Dog's Gotta Do: Dogs at Work.* New York: Henry Holt (2000).

Weisbord, Merrily, and Kim Kachanoff, D.V.M. *Dogs with Jobs: Working Dogs Around the World.* New York: Pocket Books (2000).

Read More

Farran, Christopher. *Dogs on the Job!: True Stories of Phenomenal Dogs.* New York: Avon (2003).

Jackson, Donna M. *Hero Dogs: Courageous Canines in Action.* New York: Little, Brown (2003).

Lauber, Patricia. *The True-or-False Book of Dogs.* New York: HarperCollins (2003).

Luke, Melinda. *Helping Paws: Dogs That Serve.* New York: Scholastic (2001).

Learn More Online

To learn more about dogs, visit
www.bearportpublishing.com/SmartAnimals

Index

About the Author

Meish Goldish has written more than 100 books for children.
He is doggone crazy about canines.

32